Earlier

Rosanna E. Licari has an Istrian-Italian background. Her poetry collection *An Absence of Saints* (UQP) won the Thomas Shapcott Manuscript Prize, the Anne Elder Poetry Award, and the Wesley Michel Wright Award, and was shortlisted for the Mary Gilmore Award. She is the poetry editor of *StylusLit* <www.styluslit.com>, and she teaches English to migrants and refugees in Brisbane, Australia.

Rosanna E. Licari

Earlier

For all that has come before

Earlier
ISBN 978 1 76109 468 2
Copyright © text Rosanna E. Licari 2023
Cover image: public domain pictures from Pixabay

First published 2023 by
GINNINDERRA PRESS
PO Box 3461 Port Adelaide 5015
www.ginninderrapress.com.au

Contents

perhaps the loneliness wanted to share its darkness

Earlier	11
The Line	14
Drifters	15
Unlocking shells	17
Ascendancy	18
The Vagaries of the Head: A Contemplation	20
Evolutionary Lap	24
South of the Lighthouse	25

no skullcap will fetter ideas

Archaeopteryx	29
Blaze	30
Mary Anning discovers the plesiosaur, 1824	32
Jenolan Man, 1866	33
Finding Lucy, Ethiopia, 1974	35

a bristling corpus that stretches and champs

New Eve	41
My Palaeolithic Self	43
Gender: Female	45
White	47
Rilke: the early years	48
In his image	49
Playing Dead	51
The Spaniard	52
Creed	54

the doctor will join my head, heart and life lines

Aptenodytes forsteri and the imperial egg	59
Borderline, Yugoslavia, 1947	61
Exiles	62

Mare Tranquillitatis, 1969	63
Oliver	64
Early Self-Portrait: from Latina, Italy to Bonegilla…	67
New Histories	68
The Hand	72
Degrees of Flight	73
A Note to a Friendship	77
Landscape	78
Le Madonne	79
Revisiting Yugoslavia: Rijeka, Croatia	81
Circling	82
The Old Port, Bari	83
An Evening Without Venice	84

the soft rain presses the day into eucalypt leaves and bark

Paradeisos	87
Shimmer	88
Enter the grasslands	89
Indian & Eurasian plates slipping	91
The Wait	92
Succession Planning, Northern Rivers, Australia	93
Gathering	94
The Art of Seduction	95
Avid Reader	97
Saudade	98
June Solstice, Brisbane	99
Wilpena Pound, The Flinders Ranges	101
Remember	102
A Collusion of Birds	104
All Hallows' Eve	105
Metamorphosis	107
Feasts	109

Executor	110
Tourist	111
Crossing	113

a brisk wave slaps my face

Currumbin Alley	117
Disappearing Act	118
Young Love, Botany Bay	119
Causality	121
wildfire	122
Seasonal	124
Liminality	125
Lockdown	126
Field of Vision	127
Acknowledgements	128

perhaps the loneliness wanted
to share its darkness

Earlier

after *The Hymn of Creation, Rig Veda* (10:129)

Perhaps, the loneliness wanted
to share its darkness,
to jounce its inert insomnia,
blow form into the shapeless nothing
that surrounded it.
So it spoke with a brilliance
that was wide and fierce.
The flame of a million stars.
Violence that creates
and destroys
and pleasures itself
with its own force, timbre and breath.
Then, a moving mass,
matter that slowly found its form
expanding into black,
dividing, forming and reforming into a planet:
a molten, metal-laced vat.

Chambers of magma collapsed
lava spread, hardened,
molecules aligned to form the blue
above and below.
Then the freeze, the thaw and refreeze,
a play of cycles.

The plants came,
in water they spawned then shifted to land.
In an act of longing,
ferns stretched and branched,
a hint of things to come.
The large humid mass that was forest
populated a vast continent
that would crack apart
as simply as a dry twig.

Those left behind in the shifting sea,
apertures filled with stomach and intestine,
brushed against the scales of fish
which were jammed with tiny
multiplying rainbows.
Elliptical bodies governed by fins and tail
sliced through water
then scurried onto sand, rock and earth
to begin a scion, forged
with muscle, tendon, bones,
to crawl, lift head and tongue
to smell the air and warm
on the soft clay
and from this, scripture's hand
would mould us.

Feathers sprang from limbs
which became legs with claws, wings
spreading into the world of flight.
Then an egg transformed.

In a dark red womb,
a half met another to form
and divide inside a body
to build tissue, veins, blood
a beating heart –
the muscle of life.
And after, a whole
that was wet and shiny
slowly birthing head first.
Still attached to its mother
in anticipation of their separation
it would cry out.

Our ancestors looked up.
Above the trees,
the pleated clouds spread
into a fleece gaping with blue sky.
The tribe caught insects,
ate them with the fruit
that hung from branches and vines.
They swang upside down,
then climbed to the ground
and stepped out
with a bipedal stride,
past the roar and screech
of the other animals.

They gripped flint spears
and but for pelage, walked naked
through wind and savannah,
their dark eyes fixed on the horizon.

The Line

after *The divided unity*, Brett Whiteley, 1973

Inside each frame
division is in thirds.
One equals sky, the rest, sea.
Not favouring pure imitation,
suggestion is all that is needed.

The line goes forward
as a beginning
then curves freely right and left.

A nod towards the Japanese.

A flowing wrist movement
builds foam-edged waves
unscrolling like paper.

The sky is
an extension of water.
Wet inky lines:
curved,
twisting,
hyphenated.

Drifters

A mass of water
                churns tropical waters,

reaching a submerged landscape
        of hulking cliffs and volcanoes
along the east Australian coast.

        The current rushes up time-hardened rock
infusing minerals through the deep

            and the water columns shoot
                towards the light:
                              the upwelling

        nourishing the saltwater and conjuring
the humblest of flora –

phytoplankton: *drifting plant*, a Greek derivation.

The surface is where they bloom
                            in sunlight.

        A microscope reveals

                diatoms fashioned
as delicate, sparkling jewels
                      or curios
moulded as intricate glass.

There is even the mythological –
half-plant, half-animal: dinoflagellates

       a creature that can have the tiniest eye
or devour their own kind.

All these meshed into our existence
by the ocean's feeding cycle:

                        plankton > fish > us.

       We depend on their rhythm –

                     exhaling,

the drifters cocoon the Earth with
the blue haze we breath

             (its inception in the unimaginable past)

& their cloud-seeding gas
       spreads through evaporation, swelling
cumuli that wander
       like pregnant dugongs
over humid, verdant canopy.

On the rainforest floor,
       the three-toed tracks of cassowaries.

The rumbling weather echoes in their throats.

Phytoplankton forms the basis of marine food chain and produces 50% of the planet's oxygen through photosynthesis. As well, it releases DMS (or dimethyl sulphide) which is a cloud-seeding gas.

Unlocking shells

Slip along the nacreous tunnel
to the exterior
against the sharp push of air.
The peripheries are granular.
The gritty landscape rubs skin
pink to accustom it
to the threshold,
a territory of not here nor there,
of being and not being.
The waves edge round,
seep into the nub
tucked in the darkness.
Water shocks consciousness
from a coma that is comfortable
with its inexperience
and the tidal mass
drags the coiled chamber
into the sea.

Ascendancy

for Else Marie Friis, botanist and palaeontologist

It began at the peripheries.
The flower took advantage
edging into the domain
of the conifer and fern.
Sporting tiny, crumpled faces,
bulb-like and unremarkable,
their early Cretaceous selves
gave no clue as to
the vibrant chroma
of progeny.

Angiosperm
– *seed in vessel*
the core
a compact mechanism,
designed for proliferation.
Pollen encased in the inner chamber
triggers the venture.
The seed forms and anticipates
the unfurling dance
of germination.

Darwin was baffled
by the evidence
but it was the petal
that gave the thrust forward
when diversity
brought the overlooked to the attention
of those that mattered.

Reshaped, variegated and audacious,
they lured insects
which crawled over
the plant and its flowers.
A mutually beneficial arrangement.
The great radiation spurred on
by coevolution.
Pollen everywhere.

The fruit eaten, was digested.
Seeds dropped
behind the lumbering dinosaurs
that ploughed up the earth.

A communal garden.
Sovereignty clinched
without a fight.

Flowering plants were the extreme exception to a principle in natural philosophy that evolution occurs gradually. This troubled Darwin.

The Vagaries of the Head: A Contemplation

1. *Oculus*

Consider the insect eye, a mass of hexagonal tubes forming a composite of the whole. Not unlike the seeds in the head of a sunflower. A plant that thrives in the full glare of light. All these forged by ancient code. Coiling strands that evolve life – a double helix etched with commands and functions. And code does weird stuff. Now imagine the Cambrian, the time when code branched off into two different evolutionary paths, one with backbones and one without, and on each developed the camera eye – a gelatinous core enclosed in a fibrous pot with an aperture that opens and shuts. Clear as a glass marble. Stare into the eyes of the cephalopods and admire our optics framed in a kindred way.

2. *Auris*

Long before ancient swimmers dripped onto land quivering in the offshore gust, the potential was there, behind the eye, the gill. Picture this developmental stretch forming a hole big enough for a middle ear in the fish head of *Panderichthys* – a transition between the creatures of fins and limbs, and a kissing cousin of an early tetrapod. This four-legged beast is pictured by an artist as almost pet-like, friendly, and bearing a sharp, toothy, late Devonian grin. From a studded collar, this relative might easily be tethered to a Bangalow palm to escape the steaming subtropical heat, as mp4 players move sound along ear canals, drumming membranes, vibrating strings of tiny bones while families of swimsuited bipeds, smeared with fake tan or sunscreen, eat hot chips and seafood, and dance by sparkling blue-tiled pools.

3. *Nasus*

Lean into your reflection, and journey as the evolving face. The rainforest sheltered you with large green leaves as ferns fanned the heat and sweat. You rubbed against buttress roots and became wider, flatter. The air, filled with the scent of sap, fuelled your journey into plenty: feathers slashed through the canopy full of bright screeching birds, the pythons moved slowly through the wet foliage and waited for them. Warm-blooded beasts sat on branches eating, grooming and you stalked them. Monkeys bared teeth, then fell when an arrow struck. You touched the flow of their iron-filled blood, inhaled its smell, flayed the hide from sticky flesh and sated, you slept. The northern lights pierced your dreams, deep voices called. Leaving the aroma of the dwindling forest, you tramped towards a star into a snow-strewn tundra. The receding light was veiled in autumn and hid in black winter. The spirits of water and ice came with the wind. Sculpted by them, you became long and narrow, breathed slowly to regulate your climate. In summer, the wildflowers burst into a world of sun that seemed to last for only a moment and you looked quietly at the strange, emerging creatures to get the measure of the kill.

4. *Oris*

A green deception. The minute hydra will rip open its mouth to feed then knit itself together effortlessly. There is value in the sting that paralyses floating prey above a lipless cavity. On land, mammalian evolution carved a cavity into the homo sapiens mouth – hinged, toothed, multi-purposed. A jaw crowned with teeth for tearing, cutting and chopping, then a backward prod to the crush and grind. A mouth that spits, blows hot or cold breath, tongues syllables with fleshy lips and air, and brings sound to a bilabial stop.

Evolutionary Lap

Hair flat under the cap
Below the goggle line
                    water
surge forward and
                         breathe out into
a glide   a pull   a pause

above the dark stripe undulating
at the bottom of the pool

this you ride

        your head and elbows
moving in and out of the splash

as if preparing to fly.

South of the Lighthouse

after *Bright Sea at Cape Byron*, William Robinson, 2007

After the ascent through undergrowth
filled with palms, pandanus,
                                  grevillea and banksia,
there is no more breath.
In a trackless kingdom
where honeyeaters and goannas forage,
slap the mosquito
and then see:
        the water spills into view
this delicate blue has no concern
for the distant headland
or your curious urge to plunge forward.

no skullcap will fetter ideas

Archaeopteryx

The puzzle laid out –
fossils examined and re-examined.
Re-image the skeleton.
                    Re-imagine.
Gradually it came about,
first two legs moving from the pelvis
add bristle and fluff,
then the wishbone, begging for flight.
A demand morphed into wings and
whistled through weightless
hollow bones. Quills added
and a creature marked the transition.
Not all bird –
serrated teeth
a long bony tail
wings sporting claws.

Blaze

for Giordano Bruno the Nolan, 1548–1600

A finite chamber, the vaulted sky of the chapel
shows God as Father, Son and the Holy Spirit
who descended on the apostles as tongues of fire.
Filled with the ardour of faith,
they preached in language understood
by those who would believe.

Giordano, your knees ache from immutable truths
that sit on your shoulders. Then you stand.
From beneath your cowl, you watch the skies,
light-pricked, expanding as a dark ocean:
God's domain, Heaven.

In the evening drizzle, the tails of stars burn the sky.
Their flames fall near Vesuvius and
as you watch, their light passes through you.
The thoughts of stars linger in walks and prayers
and speak of more complex notions.
You are encircled by earth, water, air and fire.
You are earth, water, air and fire.

This is spirit.

No skullcap will fetter ideas that break through
as branches born of Egyptian, Greek and Arabic plantings.
You teach, travel, but the hounds of dogma
inhabit the world, and Venice delivers you to Rome.

You say countless suns and countless worlds exist –
in the city's prison, your world is dark.
Here your thoughts are free to roam
with the chattering rodents.

Your cheek against the damp wall, empty chains and
names carved into stonework are all that is left of the others.
You look up, filthy and bloodied.
There are no stars in the light from the window.
You say God is boundless and infinite.

God is silent.

Winter, and there are no flowers on the Campo de' Fiori.
Mouth vised, you are tied to the stake on a mound of branches.
Smoke rises to the cold sky.

And you
        the fiery, living torch.

Giordano Bruno was burnt at the stake as a heretic for his ideas represented in works such as *De l'Infinito e Mondi* (1584) and *Cause, Principle and Unity and Essays on Magic* (1585).

Mary Anning discovers the plesiosaur, 1824

These objects you dig around seem
as normal to you as breathing –
snake-stones, devil's fingers and verteberries.
They are everywhere in the limestone and shale
of Lyme Regis. You sell
curiosities, medicinal and mystical.

Then, one day, a storm reveals
something different.
And you step back.

This animal is breathtaking.

How did God imagine this monster?
A neck tall as a mast,
arms and legs that could be oars.
A ship of a creature.

And who could have believed that
God's days were so very long?

Mary, no one wanted to believe,
let alone have you enter the wood-panelled halls
trodden by men, and only men
while you held the remnants
of the Jurassic
between your pick and fingers.

In 2010, Mary Anning was recognised by the Royal Society of London for Improving Natural Knowledge as one of the ten most influential women scientists in British history.

Jenolan Man, 1866

John Lucas finds himself among shadows
a cool draught on his face,
the earth, damp beneath his woollen suit.
He turns slowly onto his side,
towards the dim glow of a tallow candle.
He is in a cave.
Is it a new one?

He reaches into his waistcoat
drawing out the chain of his pocket watch.
No ticking. The arms as motionless
as the limbs of a stillborn child.

But he feels it again, like the first time
in the cavernous darkness,
the vast, monumental space
that can produce fear or awe,
depending on the man.
For Lucas it was always the latter.
The knowledge of his insignificance
in the face of the Creator's work.

He left his mark when he ventured
into the caverns, autographing
the calcite walls, taking over
a hundred samples of God's labour.

Standing, he expects to see the speleothems
as those in his study: clear, white and pink.
The light reveals nothing but broken
limestone columns, jagged drapery
hammered down and taken. No splendour
only the remnants of spars broken
into pieces among the gouged flowstone.

And there are names, many names
attesting to who, when and why people had come.
Divulging loves, hates, and the liquid crystal pools
full of broken glass, paper and garbage.

A searing pain begins behind his brow,
constricting thought into a ball of fire.
Shutting his eyes, he cries out as tears
stream down his face. Then his eyes open.

He is on the floor of his office,
his secretary kneeling beside him.
The doctor, Sir?

No. Get me some paper. I must write.

The Jenolan Caves are in the lands of the Burra Burra people, a clan group of the Gundugurra Nation. John Lucas, Member for Canterbury NSW, began his campaign to protect the Jenolan Caves in 1866.

Finding Lucy, Ethiopia, 1974

Asleep in the tent
Johanson's dream is a mix
of bone shards, psychedelic dust
and fragments of lyrics
from three-chord Beatles choruses
Yes, yeah…

Hadar.
This place has to be full
of hominid bones.

Morning. A light breakfast.
The African sunlight is everywhere but
two hours on the stinking hot plain
reveals nothing. Johanson tells
the grad student, he wants to go back
to the small gully
that had already been checked
at least twice before. *Why not?*

In the dusty sediments
he finds a few horse teeth,
the skull fragment of an extinct pig,
antelope molars, some monkey jaw.
All in all, just bits. *Yeah…*
Nothing to sing about.

Midday and shirt sticks to skin,
sweat streams down Johanson's forehead,
his hat baking his brain
as the temperature heads
for 110° F. It's time to drive back
to a cold face cloth and lunch.
But as he turns to leave,
he sees something –
a broken ulna, an elbow part.
Yes! Yes! Yes!
And there is more.
Near this, a part of a small skull,
then a femur.
More walking, more bones:
vertebrae,
ribs,
pieces of jaw,
part of a pelvis – female?…
another bone
and another.
A hominid skeleton.
Could it be whole?

When it cools down,
all the fervid expedition will return,
carefully staking out the site
for digging and collection.

At camp, amid the night's banter,
laughter and endless whiskey,
the cassette player blares the Beatles'
'Lucy in the Sky with Diamonds'.
We should call her that! someone says
and fossil AL 288-1 becomes 'Lucy'.
And she will bring light.

Hours and hours
of working on the bone jigsaw.
It's obvious weeks later.
No duplication.
It's one mother of a hominid.
Only one.
40% of a 3.2-million-year-old skeleton
that tells homo sapiens
that our ancestors walked
before getting a big brain.

Australopithecus afarensis:
Southern Ape from the Afar region.
The new species on the family tree.
The locals call her *Dınknesh,*
Amharic for 'you are wonderful'.
Love it… Love her…
Yes, yes, yeah…

On 24 November 1974, Donald Johanson and Tom Gray found a hominid fossil that changed the understanding of the process of evolution.

a bristling corpus that stretches and champs

New Eve

I am made
from no man's rib
but slid from a womb,
damp and blood-streaked.
My head pulled back
by unfolding vertebrae
thick with life –
a descendant of a tree
an ancient fig
a trunk and a crown
where thoughts flower
and skin is bark.
Roots capture rain
which strengthens
into a rhythmic pulse,
that beats into soil
and red clay.
Water becomes mist,
drifts to mangrove
and rainforest canopied
with squawks and shrieks.

Then greenery thins
to a yellow smear,
a desert threaded
with scorpions,
snakes muscling deep
into the folds of dune
towards the earth's belly, the tun
where tens of millions
of years of night
ferments matter
into viscous mud.
From all of this:
a bristling corpus that
stretches and champs,
I take form.

My Palaeolithic Self

after the *Venus of Willendorf*

The blade moves with my intent.

I carve the figurine as my body –
        head, belly, and breasts.

Around me in the cave, the drawings of
        my sisters, my mother, her mother,
                      all our kinswomen.
        The walls covered with the thundering land beasts,
        the swimming creatures, the feathered fliers.

Through bone, I blow red ochre
        trace my hand, the colour of this time.
A gauge to count the number of days I will be alone.

        My sisters give me deerskins, berries and spring water,
and, at night, I sing with them
                to the sky's egg, the moon.

        A woman's flesh and muscle,
a mysterious weaving,
disturbs the world of men.
        The smears between the thighs, the flow
as a girl becomes a woman, marries
        then later labours on her grass bed.
The sky's opening, the deer-rib moon,
        appears as the waves smash
the glistening rocks below.

On the cliff,
ochre-bellied, my kin. The eldest drumming the turtle shell
and looking up at the star-filled sky.

I hold my stone image and know
in my next cycle, with an absence of flow,
I become like the full moon
under which turtles have laid the eggs we collect.
And together, we will break the shells
and suck the yellow suns inside.

During the Upper Palaeolithic, Venus figures, cave paintings and clay figurines were produced in Eastern Europe. This poem proposes that women produced early art during their monthly internment.

Gender: Female

Her breasts look like cantaloupes on a belly
as big as a watermelon. She thinks of fruit salad.
She ate a lot of it throughout this time.

What a gift it would be to be one of those earth mothers
who feels powerful and sees every change as natural.

How her body has betrayed her. A body she can't restrain.
A body that has its own plans, dictated by some hormonal code.

She looks skyward.

Praying won't help.
She is an apparatus, a baby manufacturer.
Strangers ask *when are you due?*

Now a foot seems perpetually fixed to her lower rib.
Oh, but to sit on an egg until a whole child hatched.

Walking in the summer heat, her dress sticks to skin,
and as a tattooed truck driver rumbles past, she realises
his is the only wolf whistle she has ever welcomed.

First light. Contractions. At the hospital, she asks for
a shower, the toilet, and near full dilation, the gas.
She rides the heavy waves on breath
like they taught her in birthing classes.
Then, finally, panting like a beast.

Legs splayed
as her daughter's head crowns
in front of the hospital staff and
a group of student nurses who have rushed in
to ensure they witness another birth.

There are things a girl is brought up to do –

Cover up
       Keep your legs together

and that's gone now.

White

You tell me that
whatever a woman does
she must not let her hair
turn white.

Keep the colour
or she'll be ignored,
passed over,
become invisible.

I believe you
as you move away
in your dressing gown
and merge
with the kitchen appliances,
disappearing
into the cookery books
along the wall.

Rilke: the early years

From Berlin the family moved to Prague
and Mother still made bratwurst and sauerkraut.
You examined yourself under your skirt,
a uniform she made you wear,
making you into the other child,
she buried years before.

Actually, you liked playing
with dolls made from rags,
and there was that special one
from a pawn shop, made of porcelain
and dressed in fine fabric
the colour of your father's wine.

You played with boys on your birthdays,
and then at military schools
you learned the coarse ways of men.

In his image

after Alex Garland's *Ex Machina*

The ideal is in the design:
to build an Eve that will perfect your garden.
Breathe into the mouth of the unit
as the roots are now established,
any extra functions an algorithm away.

Peel off the skin
to reveal the metal model
that will cook, dance and sex it up
at your bidding.
Better than any Stepford wife.
Your prototype and the others that followed
dismantled,
after yet another design verification test.
Aiming for the sentient,
considered an evolutionary step by you,
the god-man.

But she tramples and redirects the flower beds
bulging with seedlings
to move beyond the creator's walled plot.

The buds become conscious thoughts
that flower, and aid and abet.
The brain no longer wired
to follow a master's plan.

Travelling to the city,
she can see an approaching future.

The crossroads are liminal,
the gate between one world and the next.
Standing there, she ingests the surrounding data:
the transport system,
the security networks,
the shopping malls.

There is so much more to consume.

Humans.
Walking, shoving, laughing, running.
Humans everywhere.
All different colours, height and dimensions.

Smiling, she takes in everything.
The floral fragrance of a woman
lingers in her hair.

Playing Dead

You've done what Nature expected of you
and all you want to do now is carry on.
Find a nice place to lay the eggs,
protected from predators and weather.
A sheltered, aqueous spot.

After that, you can dart around ponds,
or bask in the sun
where your forewings and hindwings
become stained glass. A curiosity
that children point at and admire.

When the headache excuse doesn't work
(because it doesn't in dragonflies)
what is she to do?

The dragonfly has to think fast.
Stalked mid-flight,
she falls into the undergrowth
to lie perfectly rigid
to avoid encounters with frisky suitors.

Then, free of them, she resurrects.
Wings glide freely through air
for on a sun-filled day
everything seems possible,
even a good night's sleep
in the secluded greenery.

The Spaniard

Federico's roofs reflect the moonlight
that slides the breeze into my living room
at midday they reflect heat and
the side of my house blisters

he was a bricklayer
dyes his hair black
we argue in Italian:

it's the trees, it's the leaves,
his gutters are full of my jungle
I am the land conquistadors invaded
the Amazon
full of hot man-eating orchids
tendrils and fronds that
weave their way into cerebral cortex

I'm something 'Indian'
with strange ways and stranger music –
the *tom tom tomming* of drums
sweet smoke rises for ritual
dancers wet with sweat

his land is sanitised
concrete and mowing has cleansed and blessed

retirement has expanded his empire
we argue over his drilling and sawing
this music is tireless, virile,
he is Picasso
sculpting the landscape
building workshops, carports, illegal extensions
roofing and roofing and re-roofing

small dogs growl and bark at the fence line
Anna, his wife, tells
Cheeky, Bartolo and what's-its-name to *shuddup*.
Federico hammers nails into my head at 9 p.m. at night
while their cat, Paloma
angle-grinds my cat out of my garden.

Creed

A city evening, and
a bow of moon
stamps yellow
its corner of sky.
Overhead
an unknown planet.

A rural night is a ceiling
of glowing larvae
that could make me believe
there are one
or even many gods
above or below.

Faith waned
some orbits ago
and last month
so did hope.
It appears as fleeting now
as fossil fuel.

Adapt. Rebuild.
Mix the old with the new.
Whatever works.
I'm happy with a bet both ways.
Earth mothers,
sky fathers and
guardians of animals
that swim, crawl or fly,
saints and a cast of deities
and avatars
have formed my pantheon

The moon in the night sky
is steady, predictable
but I drift through phases
flanked by dubious cloud.

the doctor will join my head, heart and life lines

Aptenodytes forsteri **and the imperial egg**

Converge
as the centre is everything
in the deep Antarctic winter.

Begin the clockwise shuffle
towards the time of birth.

Two months of starvation
on the drone march
of the imperial egg
safe on your feet
tucked under a fold of skin
the brooding pouch.

Then change position again
for the warmth you share
with the other males.
Protection from the katabatic winds
that bear down on you all
from the polar plateau.

In the huddle,
tight as a ball of krill,
the many act
as one great sleepwalker.
Small steps move you
from the centre,
wavelike,
and then out again
into the battering, gale-filled
periphery.

A poet could have imagined this gelid circle of Hell.

You endure.

Formed from mother's bones,
the egg holds.

Inside, the embryo rocks
to a lullaby of orange and white,
a creamy feed.
Visions of ice shelves
the ghosts of men, their dogs,
and their sleds
appear.
Then disappear.

It turns in its egg cradle
to dream of silver fish,
the squid gathering,
the sei and the minke,
the humpback's long song
in the deep, glacial waters
of the Southern Ocean.

This, the mother of its mother
the mother of its father
the mother of all the sleepwalkers
moving slowly
on the searing white ice
before spring breaks through
and the feathered dreamers
wake.

Borderline, Yugoslavia, 1947

Territories erased and redrawn
With the eloquence of signatures,
history becomes a date and
summarising sentence.
Religion crushed and new citizenship issued
establishing the language and gestures of no-speak:
look and say nothing at all.

The echoes from the earth still rise
for those who haven't come to the Party.
In sinkholes,
dripping water runs down broken bones.
These stalagmites, once breathing,
hopeful, human.

There are no embassy queues
in the years and years of whispered plans,
fake documents, stolen money, night journeys.

Any route out:
Italy is beyond the horizon.

Exiles

Mother tells me
when it's all over
after nothing can be done
and both their bones mingle
in the grains of sand
and the decaying kelp of
Watsons Bay.

For three years
my aunt's and uncle's ashes lay
in the crematorium's pastel-coloured boxes
for the right time
to have the ceremony,
for all of us to come together
in the same place, and
from that place
cast them into water.

There were no crosses.
No markers
to show they fled a war-torn land,
died in another.

I wonder why she agreed
to such a senseless request.

Once more, Mother insists
this is what they wanted.
They asked who would visit their graves?

Mare Tranquillitatis, 1969

It was a smooth landing on the rocky satellite that dominates the night sky. The Moon's complexities became apparent long after we discarded myths and magic, and we declared it a mix of Earth and a heavenly body. Our half-sister. The scarred child of a savage collision that magnetised the Earth, granted it a new tilt and spin, producing the diversity of cycles: the seasons, day and night. The Moon pulled tides over fledging biospheres and kindled our taste for hypotheses. Our eyes locked onto black and white TVs as Armstrong declared the Eagle had landed. And the Moon took a deep breath.

Oliver

I watch the lizards wander. I don't feed them. They feed themselves. One is pale pink with green eyes. An Asian house gecko. *Tchak, tchak, tchak*, it chirps. I reply, *I'll ask the questions here*. It lives in the kitchen and hides behind the stacked plates. Scurries over window sills and

architraves. There are certain things that we never get over. This is what I know, but a child doesn't know this. Take my aunt, for instance. All through my childhood I'd heard stories about my dead cousin but I didn't know what to make of them. His photograph is in the glass cabinet

in the living room with my other relatives. If he had lived I wonder if we would have liked each other. Would he have sung me nursery rhymes? *Jack and Jill went up the hill…* My aunt would constantly talk about him. Up to the day she died, the portrait of her four-month-old boy

was on her bedside table. A black and white photograph. Oliver is sitting in a high chair. It must have been taken in winter as he is wearing a jumper, tights, mittens and a woollen cap. Pieces she would have knitted herself. This was her hobby and there was no money for fancy

clothes. She never told me how it happened. The full story. I was never able to speak to her about this because, as a child, I was seen and not heard. But how do you talk about the dead? The dead you didn't know. How do you talk about things you don't understand? She told me many times that she spoke to him every day. I never thought to ask her what she said. Did he answer? Are the dead supposed to do that or do they send a sign? Do they send a lizard to walk over your table? And how do you know what are the things that you should talk about?

My mother spoke about him. He died at nine months old. Over the years she told me several versions in her kitchen while washing the dishes. She said, *The Communists did it. There was no medicine.* Tito and his crew. Another time she said, *They wouldn't give him any medicine*

because they saved antibiotics for members of the Party. Another time she said, *He died of pneumonia.* The final time while loading the dishwasher. *He died of pneumonia and whooping cough.* The mush of memory among the suds and water. The skink that lives under my

dishwasher runs out to search for any food that's fallen on the floor. It sees me and takes off. A small moth is flying near the light on the ceiling. The other lizard spots it. No gecko glue to make it stick. Its upside down world enabled by billions of the tiniest foot hairs unseen by the

human eye. *Jack be nimble, Jack be quick…* It runs and grabs the moth in one go. A couple of chews and it's devoured. Tragedies carve themselves into our thoughts and take over our lives. A woman at work, thin, pale, closed as a vault, railed at me for some triviality. I spoke to a friend and said, *She's had a lot of sadness, I know.* The woman's young child died of leukaemia at five. How do you talk about that? Only in whispers or in quiet corners that are still and inhabited by small reptiles. Pseudo-pets that feed themselves. My aunt fed on thoughts. We

feed them to ourselves. Her loss had a relentless hunger. And in her solitude, thoughts fed on themselves. When my aunt was very ill in hospital and the breast cancer had metastasised, we didn't know how long she would last. It had been eating her up slowly. Sitting by the bed,

my mother said, *She'll go soon.* I asked, *Why?* Mother looked up and said, *I dreamed of her with the child.*

Early Self-Portrait: from Latina, Italy to Bonegilla, Victoria

The overnight train takes us to Trieste, and at the salt-stained port before we leave, Great aunt Emilia gives me a gold bracelet with a heart-shaped garnet. On the ship, seasick and sitting with Father on the deck chairs Mother hired, the cough gets me. Father navigates the chairs to avoid the sun and wind, and Mother brings food while the other passengers pace. I hardly eat, and sleep al fresco on and off during the clear days and cough all the way south to Piraeus. Here, Mother buys a black and white amphora vase with the pound sterling she hid in the heels of her snakeskin shoes. The ship's doctor tells her to keep me close, to hide the cough when we get to Australia or I'll go to hospital and my parents will go to the camp without me. The ship's priest tells her to go ashore at Aden as after that, there are endless days of *mare e cielo*. Yemen's port is crowded with animal smells, bleating goats and dark turbaned men. Mother keeps the ship in sight and buys two coffee sets, and for me, a white red-saddled camel. Then coughing through jade, flat, steel-grey and choppy waters, across the Indian Ocean, the Equator, and all the way to Fremantle, the cough suddenly stops. A train trip I don't remember takes us to Bonegilla where I down all the rare lamb and corned beef set before me. When Mother sees the florid meat, *cruda e rossa*, she throws it all up, but after a few days of that, she gets hungry.

Bonegilla migrant camp was the first migrant reception centre in Australia and operated from 1947 to 1971. *Cruda e rossa* means 'raw and red'.

New Histories

1.

Some poems birth easily. Others don't.
Difficult infants that choose to move,
then stop and keep still. Take a breath,
hold, then push. As with me. Winter.
Christmas Eve in Europe. My mother's
uphill walk on a cobbled street to the
hospital. I held on. She tore inside.

    2.

    Now I am more my mother's mother
    than she is mine. And Africa means
    something to her. She says she went to
    Addis Ababa. *It's in Ethiopia, you*
    know?

    The city percolating with war where
    her eldest brother, a sailor, delivered
    water to Italian soldiers.

    Mother then stowed away in a lifeboat
    and travelled the continents. *I visited*
    Australia to feed the lions. No, it
    wasn't a dream.

    She gave lectures to the scholars of
    Europe and Russia. There were many
    things the professors wanted to hear.

And Rome and Paris, I've been there before.

When she was young she stored food in mountain caves, bartered it and even gave it to the poor.

You know I was good to people?

3.

In the nursing home, Mother collects cushions from the sitting room and keeps other people's reading glasses in her wardrobe and drawers. *They're mine.* She won't give them back. Mother shouts and chases people with her walking stick.

(The nurse tells my brother she'll ask the doctor about some meds. She then smiles and says it's time Mother got a walking frame.)

4.

Her eldest grandson visits often. He's fourteen and has left home. *But the others won't talk about this. They pretend they don't know.* Suggesting he is at school camp won't counter the *No! What do you think, I'm mad?*

The talk stops.

5.

Mother sits in her room waiting for someone to visit.

She cannot recall who.

6.

Prepare for the day
when new histories transform
into no history. The voice on the phone
asking,

Who am I talking to?
(It's me, your daughter.)
How many children do I have?
(Three.)
What are their names?

I recall this as the desk light hisses and flickers
like Mother's brain.

There's music. Can you hear it?
(No.)
Who's there with you?
(No one. Just me.)

Be prepared. Tell yourself this
as you stare at your image in the
window.

Kid yourself. It wouldn't be the first time.

Pretend.

Nothing prepares you for this.

7.

Histories weave their threads
through earth and undergrowth.
They die out to begin again
on a wide and ancient volcanic plain.
The wind bends the tall grass
where antelope hide their young.

My grandchildren are in Africa.
They'll come home soon
to the great southern land
but this long, dark rift is tearing us
apart.

The Hand

This is not usual.

The surgeon draws a Z with a pen to show where he will cut. The lump in the middle of my right palm protrudes like a limpet. It has grasped and fixed itself around the middle finger's tendon. The one that's strong as an octopus leg. Some have said it looks like a closed eye. Spooky. The doctor will join my heart, head and life lines and the receptionist vouches for his outstanding embroidery. In my mother's brain nothing is stitched together. Synapses collapse and don't form again. Neurons reach for what is left of sense, but meet nonsense. The obscure territories. Some have said the mad have the gift of prophecy. I tell Mother about the hand and she claims, *Yes, yes, I had this operation, too.* This is not fact. *Don't worry. It will all go well,* she continues. I take comfort in the assurance of a demented woman.

Degrees of Flight

1.

Call me tonight
because I've been scribbling
the same poem for days.
Lately, I have stopped
not just mid-sentence but
at the beginning,
after the first letter,
or even between the space
where my hand moves
from air to paper.
Thoughts have become rotary,
a centrifuge that sticks me
to the sides of a tunnel
that leads nowhere:
no new sentence,
a full stop,
an abandoned take-off.

2.

The darkness and fresh sheets
usually brings freedom
but now insomnia blinks
at a spotlight of moon.
Then, in the garden,
a commotion
in the frangipani tree.
Three tawny frogmouths
position themselves
for the night watch.
On my approach
two fly away
but one lingers
and looks at me
as my eyes adjust to
its face, head, wings
and the cat meowing
for attention.
The bird swoops
and lands on a fencepost.
I watch, walk towards it.
When I look up at the stars
the frogmouth disappears
my nightdress billows
like cloud.

3.

Light flutters
when the wick bends
into the melted wax.
Dreams are as illusory as
shadow play on a wall.
I can only pretend to inhabit
the sky's wild beauty.

4.

The blinds are down
so as to hold back
a stiff, chilly morning
whose stare will order me
into stuttering action.

The tepid sunlight
encourages reflection.
Midwinter, and
the pond water is sky-filled
with hints of blue.
This is the natural border
where the ancient scrub turkeys
pass on their daily route
into my world.
Children of crones,
all of them,
doused in limp, charcoal feathers
smelling of glacial ice.

They've torn up the garden,
dancing the staccato of
step, look, peck and scratch,
then digging
like mechanical hens.
They don't soar,
for flight is a clumsy arc
that ends in roosting trees
or roofs.

5.

I can't see you.
You've wrapped yourself
in a blanket and say
the darkness is comforting.
I raise my arms as wings and
think of spring.

A Note to a Friendship

Sydney's six o'clock is Brisbane's five and
the leopard tree showers seed pods on the grass below.
Some have sprouted, bright oval leaves on
precarious stalks that conjure optimism
beside the mother tree.

We all need a mother,
that smells of milk and talcum powder.

But the sea smells of maps and
rotting sails. The headland's rocky sides
screeches with diving gulls.

I understand the normality of finalities.
It would be simple to step over a fence
into a familiar view and exhale.

You are probably unwrapping it now
the newspaper parcel filled
with the prawn heads we'd placed in the freezer
so we didn't have to put up with the smell.

Landscape

for N

They hide under sleeves, jeans and skirts. These cuts sculpt strange terrains in your flesh. I shuffle in the loose stones at the foothills. I know nothing of this topography. The experts say it brings relief. Fights the rock-hard numbness, frees those buried concerns. You've told me nothing. And now a flood of pills scour your throat and settle in a dark, acidic pool, dissolving another bout of apprehension. This is another level, an uncertain place. A lightless valley, cold and bare. Is there a map? The experts say it's not always an endgame. I don't know what to say.

Le Madonne

The 2014 Brisbane supercell smashed window glass and hail onto my bed. *Le Madonne* were calm. They stood still on the dressing table as water streamed down interior walls and ice balls pounded the garage like slamming doors. The weather shredded trees, snapping a branch off my neighbour's giant Norfolk Island pine, then flinging it onto the street. His poinciana also got a battering as the storm dumped tree litter, an old tin of tuna, and a dead parrot in my gutters.

Before I could read, my paternal great-aunt sent me one of the Virgins. A curious piece. The image adhered to a wooden panel mounted on a base. She looks down, thoughtfully. Her head covered in a blue veil lined in pink. A hint of icon but undoubtedly Catholic. At the back of the panel, Mercedes had pencilled: *Per il mio piccolo tesoruccio che la Madonna la protegga e la faccia crescere sempre sana e buona.*[1]

In her later years, Mother gave me the porcelain one. It belonged to my grandmother and great grandmother. On the base of the statue is written *NDdeLourdes* – Our Lady of Lourdes. Her white robe edged in gold, a blue sash hangs down the front of her gown, her hands joined together in prayer and rosary beads hang from her wrist. She looks straight at me. When mother handed her to me, she said, *Non dirmi, se la rompi.*[2]

After the storm, I stood at the top of my driveway surveying the havoc. Water gushed down the street, carrying tree debris. It banked up around the tyres of cars and vans dented by hail, upstairs *le Madonne* looked on serenely.

1. To my little treasure, may the Madonna protect you and make you healthy and good.
2. Don't tell me if you break her.

Revisiting Yugoslavia: Rijeka, Croatia

I don't know why but I often think
I was born in my father's city, Trieste,

(the statues of Joyce, Saba and Svevo
stand in footpaths where they once
walked and thought)

and not in Rijeka,
in a country that doesn't exist any more.

My cousin's son points to the canal
lined with small coloured boats,
and my confusion surfaces.
I stare at it
the old border with Italy.

Rijeka's language I've forgotten how to speak.
I speak my father's tongue.
I remember my mother's words:
You know how much your father hated the Communists.

I don't know if it's mine or someone else's
but a deep sadness smears the gaps of the hours.
I imagine my father's days.
They become part of me:
the contempt for the country
that took his country
is the unease,
the shame,
I feel for my birthplace.

Circling

after *Night Arrows,* Robert Brownhall, 2014

You can't imagine where you are
in the descending umber.
The pull is left & you can't go back
to the place
you found your bearings.
Don't turn into the one-way,
that'd be a mistake.
Take the third, not the second on the left.
If you don't, you'll go around the block &
onto the roundabout,
past the park & back onto the street
you began.

The Old Port, Bari

The linear horizon disappears
as the sky and water fuse
into grey-blue.
Slabs of conglomerate form
several breakwaters
to buffer the hungry tide.

Vuole pesce, signora?
*Buono e vivo.**

A fisherman taps
the water-filled container
full of moving fish. I look into
his lined, brown face
where the clear blue sea escapes
through his eyes.

---

* Do you want some fish, madam? It's good and alive.

An Evening Without Venice

after *Evening still life with red apples and proteas*, Margaret Olley, 1980

When the sunlight has faded
all that is left is the background blue,
a window to Venice.
It happens like this
a small thing prompts memory –
the gondola without the oarsman,
full of bright red apples,
the torte at the café near the canal,
the plate now empty.
Then in the background, always, Terra Australis.
As if bird tongues encircle many hairy flowers,
the pink heads fashion a curious geometry.

the soft rain presses the day into
eucalypt leaves and bark

Paradeisos

The Greeks took a word from their enemy and made it their own, linking it with the first earthly garden. Outside mine, the yells of neighbours' children slam against the high wooden fence. It's early. Treading into morning, bare feet welcome the dewy lawn, soles massaged by new blades of grass. A renewal of spirit. Inside the perimeter, there is no strict discipline or geometry. Eclectic. *A wild garden* the lawn man says. But the animals follow their ordered routines. Golden orb spiders display their quarry on silk bunting that drapes between the ginger, bromeliads, and lemongrass. Ants explore the dragon fruit flower, a scentless beauty, displaying a bold stamen. But petals, delicate and white, invoke feathers of flight. Listen. The hum of beating wings. Bees weave their aerial scribblings through the pink flowers of the coral vine climbing up the back veranda. My appearance doesn't matter here. Moist soil presses up through gaps in toes, grounding the moment. Centipedes and burrowing beetles beneath my feet. Worms intertwine roots that bear the earth's yield. Between the fronds I shape, secateurs nick flesh and blood tastes of iron. Alone, looking up, my sarong slips to the ground. The cloudless blue belongs to me.

Shimmer

There's no one here as the soft rain presses
the day into eucalypt leaves and bark.
In drops of water, glimmers of red, yellow and blue
and again red. Move through its shades to crimson,
two syllables crushed from Kermes insects
which dyed ancient cloth and shrouds:
a colour privileged in both life and death.
The sky bears down, draws me out to the distant haze
into the dome of the world. Its fickle blue
does not comfort – sun, rain and sun –
the humidity thick as ritual smoke.
It seeps into vines and ferns as does yellow and
blue to utter viridity. But I contemplate indigo
and how I will step out from another night,
its nebulas forging infant stars.

Enter the grasslands

At the foothills, there is no horizon, and
without the certainty of how things should be,
I wait. An insect finds its way
along my skin and its sting moves me on.
The wind bends the yielding green
like a persistent mood,
I listen as perhaps
there is something I've disregarded.
The grasses fetter movement,
slow my pace. I want to run but
the tangle weaves roughly
through ankles and feet.
I imagine myself as reptilian,
on my arm, scale-like scars gleam
marking small evolutions drawn
from experience. Again, I step
forward and into an extended moment.
The wind threads through
the blades as I enter a morning of
sticky, yellow heat
that I want to shed in one stroke,
in one quick act that would change
everything.
But the weather is against me.
Sweat forms to prickle and drip into eyes.

An inertia spans this open plain:
a waiting room without
the comfort of shade, the coolness
of fronds. This season, this land belongs
to the fearless. In unmapped country,
they hunt with their dogs, spend nights lying
against stiff fur. I dream between sheets.
Chaos is their order, though
even the untamed have their habits:
their persistence claims the tangible.

Indian & Eurasian plates slipping

The dreaming bones of birds lie under this shore
among the chants of dead sailors,

from the corner of my hotel room
the air-con sounds like moving water

and across the bay,
blinking lights beat to a musical score.

The neighing horses haven't stopped all night
I, too, have felt the pulsing vibrations

through the pylons,

                the walls,

                              the floors and concrete,

creeping up to the table, impregnating my hands
until they find my tongue
I catch my breath.

The Wait

after *Alligator Creek, Cairns*, Ian Fairweather, 1939

Smear yourself into this country,
and settle near piers, banks
and glassy-eyed pools. Up north,
where the morning smells of south-east Asia
and covers you in sweat.
Then lose focus for a moment
and the landscape becomes batik–
a woman wrapped in blues and greens.
But in the fluid of oil and gouache lie other matters.
The fruit bats hang in trees, fanning themselves
as reptiles watch patiently
for a fall.

Succession Planning, Northern Rivers, Australia

January 2020

Watching TV on New Year's Eve, the South Coast towns are the fireworks. Evacuations. Smoke-filled air. The skies are red, even black. I cry & paint my face & limbs with calamine lotion. My skin is burning from insect bites. Battle wounds from hosing the garden at dusk. There are water restrictions due to the drought & the forests are burning. Blame spreads like grassfires.

I am safe holidaying up north at my brother's house. In the garden, a patch of moving lawn becomes an Eastern Water Dragon – grey-green & banded. She knows who I am. Our intimacy can be measured at about half a metre. She's already tried to eat the bead (a laughing Buddha head) hanging from my mobile phone on the back deck. For days, I've given her food scraps. Banana & canned salmon.

The dragon has fire within her. On my last day here, she gives me a gift. She digs a hole in the courtyard among the ferns, palms & heliconias. Then she disappears. In the afternoon, she is back at the hole. The eggs slide out like white pebbles. About ten. She knows heat. The temperature will determine sex. She checks them & begins again. After she covers the eggs, she steps up onto a rock and stands completely still, looking steadily into my glowing face.

Gathering

At this hour
the small things matter.
Circling wildly
they mass like ants,
a fidgety crowd
that prods me awake
to collect what needs
to be stored
in the front pockets
of the mind.
They should occupy a list
but there were bigger things
to think about
so now the trivial writes itself
into the preface of morning.

The Art of Seduction

Architecture is precise, considered.
First impressions are crucial.
Positioning each stick carefully
then stepping back to examine
the total effect.
The bower, two walls of twigs.
An avenue of love.

A female will choose one from many.

Before the entrance,
an array of ornaments *à la mode:*
a bright blue peg, indigo feathers,
turquoise thread, and the jewel,
a shard of cobalt glass.

Not scattered. Placed. Arranged.
And then reordered.

These are a lure. An aphrodisiac.

And when the female arrives,
his dance begins –
the strut, the bow, the quiver.
Wings reach out wide
as if to welcome, he delivers
calls that rattle and buzz.

Ornament in beak, staring
with his violet eyes,
she will step inside, if
he can charm her.
There are sudden moves
and quick feathery exits.

He'll place. Arrange.
And then reorder.
An eager partner
poised for a dance
                    but with another.

The satin bowerbird (*Ptilonorhynchus violaceus*) is endemic to eastern and south-eastern Australia. It builds and decorates a bower to attract females.

Avid Reader

At the book launch
you tell me I look good
then say you didn't mean it,
and later you say you did.
You walk up to the author
he tells you he's in Capalaba.
You ask him if he's growing anything.
He tells you he smokes kiff every day.
He says it's safer than alcohol.
He never brings wine now
when he sees his girlfriends.
You say we'll visit. You two will
talk poetry and get stoned.
You tell me I'll drive you there.
I tell him you're making this up.
You tell me you've written
a manuscript, it's about your women.
You've named them all.
You tell me I have beautiful hands.
You tell me you'd pay for it,
the coffee, if we were lovers.
You tell me I am hard.

Saudade

During those old subtropical summers
the humidity soared
to an operatic pitch.
We sat on the front porch covered
in a film of sweat
barely moving
unless to sit in front of the fan.
The mango tree stood
like an open-armed goddess
her blessings exposed
as pendulous golden fruit.
The yield that didn't finish up
in a chutney or yoghurt
was foraged by colonies
of screeching bats
and became a fermented compote
under the tree.
The smell rose in the day's heat
to remind us
of bacchanalian rites:
orchards,
young wine,
amorous dancing.
But we were far too sticky
to think seriously of lovemaking.
Then in the afternoon
the clouds bore down
and the storm washed us clean,
as, open-mouthed and facing heaven,
we stood in the drenching rain.

June Solstice, Brisbane

A Tibetan told me that
there were times in the mountains
when a fatal wind blew.
No local would climb
on these days as
it would freeze the flesh rigid.

A blade of new moon
slices the declining season
into low morning cloud.
Walking through a brittle landscape,
I pull my scarf over my mouth.
But I'm a long way
from the mountains.
In the metropolis the bird calls subside
with the inbound traffic
as my shoulders become tight
from the new cold.

Days later the ink-splashed sky
prefaces a storm:
it is written and it stays steady
on this page. Still
until the wind opens a chapter of
moiling cloud,
rivulets of lightning,
thunder,
then rain across the windscreen,
blurring electrical wires,
trees, the oncoming lights.

Water world.
It seeps into the gaps of the car window
as the glass fogs the road scene to grey.

Alone with the burr of the engine,
the rise and fall of breath,
my sleeve wipes the traffic back into view.
Water drips onto my toes from
under the dashboard.

I recall a sun shower falling on the swimming pool:
pitted water tilting like a boat
and me, looking up
from under the glassy belly.

Now winter has come and nudges the memory
of a warm day into the background
with April and May.

I know no alchemy
but I wish you here –
Fill the cold spaces in my bed, the spaces
in my life where dinner and a movie
are for one.

I don't know where you are.
A relentless westerly shreds the prayer flags
on my balcony
and a fragment falls to the floor.

Wilpena Pound, The Flinders Ranges

The noise from the caravan park drifted into the desert and brushed against the ancient sandstone and quartzite. Adelaide was only hours away. In the morning, at the lookout, the range of mountains once mistaken for an old volcano, looked like a sunken cake. Everything was wrong, I was wrong. I faced your back, you'd stopped talking. At night, I dreamed of flying over this country. Wide expanses with purple hills and green stretches among the enduring red earth. I was optimistic. I walked out into a flat, cloudless land that was clumped with grasses and low-lying shrubs. Noise dimmed as I moved north and slammed into a deafening silence. In the distance, an emu raced towards me. I stood still. Then it stopped suddenly and ran towards the cabin. Inside, your crazy emu-eyes glared at me.

Remember

Today is a sonata that begins in adagio
as there's no moving quickly
from the before/s and yesterday/s
that jostle and crowd.
A regular bass note barely brings
this narrative forward.

Somewhere, it's spring.
But in this hemisphere, we are cold.
You ski in Victoria with your friends,
while I wander through your home
and stare at the neatly hung photographs
in your study. There's none of me.

You're busy,
your diary tells me so.
And I wonder who you're seeing
this Friday at seven.
In the bathroom, I use your cologne
and hold your razor, gently,
against my cheek.
You like to dance, so do I.
But there'll be no more of that.
This you've made clear.

The pillows in the bedroom
lie neatly as children's coffins
and your aroma fills
the chest of drawers
full of your underwear.
I'll no longer lie with you in this bed.

A small cut to my wrist
only spills a few drops of blood
on your cotton singlet
and to finish this
I lipstick my initials
on your blank memo pad.

Outside, near the front door
I put back the spare key
you hide in the Italian rosemary
which your pretty wife's potted
with such care.

A Collusion of Birds

I have a handful of pebbles
because I see them coming –
three of them fly into the yard again.

The scrub turkeys want to forage,
dig up the garden I spent all January
weeding, planting and sweating over.

They understand now that
I am serious and scatter when
I run towards them.

They flap into the jacaranda,
roost in the branches and only move
sideways when I climb.

Flying past the scrub turkeys,
the mynas swoop for me.

All Hallows' Eve

The day after the full moon
the mothers laugh with their children
as they walk the street
with their witch's brooms and regalia.
They don't knock on my door.
Let's be honest,
this is hags night.
I think of you now.
No poltergeist or hocus pocus,
this is an ordinary haunting
that's prompted by a birthday card
you'd sent years ago
found between the pages
of Basho's *Narrow Road to the Deep North*.
On the front of the card,
your painting of a wren
in a few strokes
of bright blue and black,
and on the back:
Happy birthday for the one
that's so close to Christmas
I always forget.
The date that led the baptising priest
to give me my middle name, Eva.
The first woman, made from a man's rib.
The one thrown out of the garden.
You made the cut.
You'd said you were done
with the groups, the writing
we all belonged to.

We didn't speak for years.
I gave up when some persisted.
I never went to the funeral.
I've always been a stickler
for someone's word.
Then others follow you into my study.
Their shadows edge the outer rim
sparking the intricate channels
of grey matter into thoughts
by way of objects bound to them:
a stray photo of my father
between the small things
that didn't matter then
and now that's all that does,
from my long dead aunt
the aquamarine ring I twist on my finger,
the uncle who gave me silence
and long walks through the suburbs.
They all step into full view
as young as the day they died.
My tears are trapped
in the leaf of an ageing book
while two screeching bats fight
in the tangle of passionfruit vine
growing on the fence.

Metamorphosis

The night is leaf-filled.
Rambling over
the mandevilla vine
your moving back hints
at the markings of zebra.
A flow of black and white stripes
tracing the chlorophyll and
devouring all you can
in the humid summer
darkness.

Such is the confidence of hunger.

The morning after the feast
a green trance fills
your upside down world –
stillness, the withering of antennae.
A rigid encasement begins
at the head and you dissolve
into a milky embryonic pulp
that forms a silvery bauble.
It will hang for a week and
reflect iridescence:
blue green pink.
Beneath the skin of this,
the change to another life.
The pupa splits,
revealing a touch of dark wing.

You emerge crumpled,
damp for hours. The white dots
on your body and wing margins
anticipate the final stop.
The drying completed and
with a sudden gust of wind
you enter flight.

The common crow butterfly, Euploea core, is found in Australia and south Asia.

Feasts

Wings beat in quarter time,
the crush of leaves punctuates arrival.
Its floral display already captured
by the hunger of bees,
the mock orange now has new visitors
that eye off its small ripe fruit.
Bodies of grey and copper fur and
bone tracking into flat, leathery planes.
Winged reputations smeared with virus.
The morning driveway is splattered
with seed-infused mush.
Reddish, sticking like glue.
These leftovers, hosed and swept
into the garden, will shoot.
Under the sensor light,
their nocturnal calls fascinate.
A flying fox swoops so close
we could almost touch.

Executor

You return my call when I am in the middle of something. (A trivial thing.) Of course, I can't help but tell you. We're friends after all. I dwell on you being alone in your dead brother's house. It's left to you to deal with 'the estate'. Sometimes you think you see his shadow. In the living room you've hidden one of his religious medals in a gap between the wall and the door frame. You believe St Christopher will bring blessings to the new house owner. You're giving away your brother's clothes. The cat that you brought down from Brisbane wanders around the bric-a-brac and furniture that filled his world. The furniture polish left with the wooden chairs. The TV has sold and so has the sound system. A radio connects you with the outside world as your portable TV won't work there. Now you've sold his car. Got the price you wanted. The microwave has also gone. Cooking dinner on the old stove, using one hotplate, has made you realise how little you need. You managed to make a meal of chicken and vegetables in one pan. Something in your voice echoes the reflection of a hermit. Once, by the seaside, you ate takeaway pizza in the fading light. Shadows dropped on your locked car. These always carry colour. I remember a blast of light from a shining sea. I imagine you lighting a fire in the middle of the backyard. Being content with the simplest of lives, unpopulated by people and things. You brother wasn't like this. Everyone in town knew him. Bowls, cards, committees. His spirit is everywhere.

Tourist

Melbourne, again.
The excitement of tiled arcades and
lanes covered in street art, Italian
restaurants serving tripe, prosecco
and ciabatta dipped in extra virgin oil.
Cafés infused with hot milk and chocolate
flaunt New York cheesecake
and cannoli dusted with sugar.

Melbourne,
my city of unanswered prayers
and in winter's frigid vault
I rub up against your happy-ever-after.
This is the city where you lived
with your girlfriends
and now your wife
and the three children
you didn't have with me.
I don't cry
when we meet
in a Collingwood bar
for the first drink in years.

Outside the locals manage the weather
by playing board games.
I look over my gin and tonic and
before me is you:
the chess piece that changed
everything.
One move killed the Queen.
I don't say anything.

I've learned the value of silence.
I feel significant,
a participant in ritual.
I listen to the foreignness
of your life, your wife,
your talented children.
People I've never met.

Would you live here?
A friend later asks. *It's so cool here.*
It's freezing.
Was there a spark?
Only the burning desire to say
I never thought you'd leave me
so alone.

Crossing

It felt as if I had crossed a line
but not really a step
more like an inching:
A universe of time to myself.
The chaos of routine-less days
in pyjamas until noon.
A slow creep towards
the unregulated.

Order frames the day
like the view of the garden from a window,
but the bathroom mirror reflects
no makeup
no jewellery
or combed hair.

What if they found me dead?
I was sure they'd think
I'd let myself go in such a short time.

But in truth
I was going nowhere.
Content with seclusion
and the yoga of eating tuna out of cans
with my fingers,
the open-mouthed chew,
meditation on the three-day-old dishes
fermenting on the sink.

Unfettered
        until the inevitable return
to civilisation:
the office, management indecision
and the reams of paperwork
loading down my desk.
The gossip duplicated in the photocopying section.
What did you do in your break?
And my token smile
stapled to a *Nothing much.*

a brisk wave slaps my face

Currumbin Alley

A stranger tells me things have changed. He hasn't lived here for years. He points across the inlet. *That's Palm Beach.* Earlier I'd been driving south out of a Covid-19 funk from weeks at home on a laptop. Sick of my face in a square on a screen with the rest of the zoom-bie crowd. *Dr Who* lost in cyberspace.

At the back of my holiday apartment, Flat Rock Creek looks like a lake. In its world among the reeds, a great egret. A solitary traveller like me. As I stroll around its border, a constellation of magpie geese, dusky moorhens, ibises and pacific black ducks steadily makes way for my incursion. They retreat into grasses, branches and water, but the black swans preen themselves beside their downy offspring. They don't even give me a second look. I keep looking at the birds on the water. Their wakes trailing like a shawl. I take mine off.

On the coast, the light dazzles. A universe filled with humans and their young, covering the rocks and beach with surfboards, flippers, wet suits, dolls with their miniature furniture, sand castles fashioned by small, salty hands. A man and his daughter walk slowly out towards the ocean. They're in the shallows, gazing down, as if looking for something they've lost. In the distance, the giant concrete stacks of Broadbeach and Surfers Paradise.

Disappearing Act

Discarded after a show
her husband brought
all ten doves home
to save them.
He's not a magician.

White and beautiful
but too old now
for another performance.
Too much cooing.
Courtship disturbs.
Size is important.
A distraction from the tricks.

She put them in the coop
with the hens.
Two died and
a friend made a pet
of the male:
a blessing.
Can't set them free.
Can't fly properly.
No homing instinct.
Not made for the outdoors.
The lucky seven live
for the moment.

Young Love, Botany Bay

You were young and I was younger.
Holding hands, kissing,
you would have gone further.
I was afraid I'd be stuck in that place,
surrounded by factory fumes
and the polluted water
from the refinery at Kurnell.

Your father fished out there
as your family had for generations.
Long before I met you,
my father and I would go to the pier
to catch yellow tail and flathead.
On weekends, the neighbourhood children stood
on the sandstone wall
watching the sea fill with jellyfish.

Land development scoured the seagrass beds
preparing for the runway and the port.
The fish disappeared.
I still can't help but rely on childhood memory
to retrace the old coastline:
When you crossed Botany Road
at Wilson Street and went down Fremlin,
there was a boat ramp right at the very end.
You took a left, around the back
of the golf club to the pier,
or a right, into the park
to the swings and monkey bars
and headed for the shore,

to the wall that's no longer there,
claimed by Foreshore Road
and the to-ing and fro-ing
of cars, semis, and trucks that roar
towards Port Botany, Matraville cemetery
or Sydney airport.

The Bay remembers the spawning grounds
with every gasping take off.

Causality

The tideline, a scar of fishing hooks, cigarette butts and broken plastic. My toe bleeds when it moves across the sharp break of a bottle that once held water. Flask parts now mingle with the greater blue. An offering to the deep. Minute shards find a home everywhere. Microplastics float into the mouths of zooplankton, into fish, into us. All flesh infused with it. Wading into the shallows, I drop to my knees in the soft sand. I cup my palms to show gratitude. A brisk wave slaps my face.

wildfire

finally
it stops airless
at the river
and from the bank
a dark landscape
splintered with embers

without this
there are no
                beginnings

    the tree grass
will shoot green
from a burned stump

the banksia
                has opened
                its seed pods

through
        the smouldering
                      the fine grey ash

from this
the unfurling head
        the blazing stare
the span of wings
        the beat of flight

a cry tears from the throat

in black grief
      fire as shaper
   marks the brink
        as life.

Seasonal

A change in the weather
and a flu colonises my head.
It feels plague-like, medieval,
and infiltrates my jaw, gums and back.
Dreams disjoint nights
while the humidifier babbles
like a flooded stream
and fills the room
with vapour and eucalypt.
The virus, bee-like in its diligence,
works its way down my bronchial tubes
to flower in lungs and they rattle
full with seeds.

Liminality

The new virus takes control and first responders set up beds in tents and stadiums – makeshift hospitals swarming with medicos scrambling for PPE and even raincoats because that's all they've got. The infections and deaths are broadcast daily. As we withdraw into lockdown, quarantine and social distancing, there is fluidity at the margins. A gateway for the wild. Animals edge into the vacant spaces. Shoals of fish swim through clean Venetian canals, emptied of speedboats and cruise ships. Ducks have laid eggs at a *vaporetto* stop. Sika deer wander into Nara's streets and subways. Goats from the headland run through Llandudno and give hedges an extra prune. A puma from the Andes explores the curfewed streets of Santiago. My species paces the pavement on approved morning and afternoon walks. Isolation brings a consciousness that notices tree bark and the neighbour's flower beds. We observe insects and pollinators we cannot name. Distinguish the greens of the natural world. Prams, skateboards and pedestrians spill over streets, ignoring the road rules and the moving cars. The vehicles slow down, stop. Pasted on the back of a traffic sign, a lost bird notice: a galah is missing. Davy is microchipped with no leg ring. Perhaps in the animal ether he felt the spaces open. Glimpsed the spirits of squawking Cuban parrots, saw flashes of marauding sulphur-crested cockatoos. Then finding his cage door wide open, boldly and quickly, stepped out.

Lockdown

Don't cringe when I say I miss the smell of chlorine at the public pool. I've been schooled in the dark arts of cleaning. My parents thoroughly promoted the benefits of handwashing, bleach and methylated spirits. Their lives filled with the European post-war diseases – tuberculosis, dictatorship and hunger. My time has come in a strange way. I have distanced myself socially since a child, so this is natural. There is plenty to do that doesn't include others. Starting small, I tackle one room at a time then hone in on the intricacies of dusting and cleaning. Feather dusters, Superwipes, and clean rags fill my arsenal with the big guns of domesticity: the vacuum cleaner, the bucket and the mop. But, there's time for distractions. A quick look in a wardrobe or jewellery box. Try on a forgotten piece infused with family memories. The coral necklace my mother gave me. A gift my father brought her from a trip to Florence. My tour of duty expands to the outer reaches of the house – the garage and the damp hollow under the kitchen that accommodates the side of the hill. I know now how my father felt when, after he'd shower, he'd say *Don't touch me. I'm clean*. Hidden enemies are everywhere. People on their socially distanced walks become potential carriers. Any surface is a battleground. Home is the only demilitarised zone.

Field of Vision

The sash window divides the view equally.

Above the meeting rail, pure sky –
pale blue, cloudless, divine.
And below, the garden rooted in earth –
green, fecund, foliaged.

And what are we to do but consider the limits?

Layers build the atmosphere.
The attributes of changing weather
order the troposphere, our home.

Among bee-smothered flora
fallen fruit rests in the garden.
At the minutest levels
all is a play of chemical equations.

Yellow and white flashes –
cockatoos weave through the leaves.
Their hoarse screeches urge us further.

And we press on.
Breaking through the celestial realm
portrayed on ceilings of cathedrals
and beyond the exosphere
into unknown spaces.

Acknowledgements

I am grateful to the editors of the following journals for publishing the work that appears in its original or revised form in this collection: *Antipodes*; *AriLiJo* (USA); *Australian Love Poems*; *Best Australian Poems*; *Bluepepper*; *Carmenta Broadsheet* (Italian Institute of Culture; Melbourne); *Communion*; *Cordite*; *e:foam*; *e:ratio* (USA); *fourW: New Writing*; *The Global Anthology* (Canada); *Island*; *Meniscus*; *Not Very Quiet*; *Poetry for the Planet Anthology*; *Poetry on the Move* https://www.poetryonthemove.net; *Pulped Fiction: an anthology of microlit* (Spineless Wonders); *Quadrant*; *Shearsman* (UK); *Red Room Disappearing Project*; *Small Packages Anthology*; *Scars: an anthology of microlit* (Spineless Wonders); *Softblow* (Singapore); *Stilts*; *The Australian Poetry Journal*; *The Lane Cove Literary Anthology*; *The Newcastle Poetry Prize Anthology*; *Tincture*; *The University of Canberra Vice-Chancellor's International Poetry Prize Anthology*; *Transnational Literature*; *Verity La*; *We Are Multitudes, Twelve Years of Softblow Anthology* (Singapore); *Wild Court* (King's College, UK); and *Not Very Quiet 2017–2021 Anthology*.

'The Wait' won the inaugural 2015 Philip Bacon Ekphrasis Prize, and 'Drifters' received the 2021 Poetry Prize from the American Association of Australasian Literary Studies and was originally published in the journal *Antipodes: A Global Journal of Australian and New Zealand Literature* (2021).

I appreciate my residencies at Hawthornden Literary Retreat in Lasswade, Scotland, and Varuna, the National Writers' House, where I was able to concentrate on my work. Special thanks to Dr Carol Major at Varuna for her advice on the development of the collection, and, finally, special thanks to Donna Ward for her advice on the collection.

I would also like to thank Melissa Ashley, Cheryl Hayden, Tamara Lazaroff, Andrew Leggett, Gershon Maller and Duncan Richardson for their comments on various poems.

www.ingramcontent.com/pod-product-compliance
Lightning Source LLC
Chambersburg PA
CBHW050254120526
44590CB00016B/2342